WELCOME TO THE CHURCH

LAY ACTION MINISTRY PROGRAM
7200 E. DRY CREEK ROAD, SUITE D-202
ENGLEWOOD, CO 80112

Cook

800-323-7543

Welcome to the Church © 1987 by Lay Action Ministry Program, Inc.

Scripture quotations, unless otherwise noted, are taken from the Holy Bible: New International Version, © 1973, 1978, 1984 by the International Bible Society, used by permission of Zondervan Bible Publishers.

93 92 91 90 89   5   4   3   2

David C. Cook Publishing Co.
850 North Grove Avenue
Elgin, IL 60120
Printed in U.S.A.

Editor: Gary Wilde
Designer: Chris Patchel
Cover: Lois Rosio Sprague

ISBN: 0-89191-514-1
Library of Congress Catalog Number: 86-72607

TABLE OF
CONTENTS

LAY ACTION
MINISTRY PROGRAM

LAMP courses are based on the HEAD, HEART, and HANDS approach to learning. HEAD represents Bible *content* that you want to know. HEART represents your *personal application* of the truth. HANDS refers to the LAMP goal of preparing you to *use course content in the lives of other people*—imparting to others what you have learned (see II Tim. 2:2).

A thriving and fruitful Christian experience needs roots that extend deep into the soil of God's truth. *Welcome to the Church* provides such fertile ground by examining foundational truth about the salvation experience, God, humanity, spiritual warfare, and local church involvement. When learners know these basics, they can fit into the life of the church as God intended.

Course Requirements

This course is for every Christian who is willing to put forth the effort in personal study. But we want you to know "up front" what it is going to cost you in terms of time and commitment. *It is going to cost you a good hour of home study for each lesson.* Make every effort to spend this much time as a minimum requirement.

How to Use This Course

Though you may complete the course by yourself, you will normally be preparing for a weekly group meeting. In this meeting you will be an active participant because of your personal study. One lesson is to be completed each week, prior to coming to the weekly group meeting.

The weekly group meeting for this course features a discussion of the lesson that you have studied during the week. It also includes other elements to encourage group life, and to guide group members toward personal application of the material. The meeting, planned for at least one full hour, should be led by a person who enjoys leading discussions and helping people learn. The study leader will study the lesson in the same way as anyone else in the group. In addition, a **Leader's Guide** is available, with specific suggestions for conducting each weekly group meeting. This **Leader's Guide** can be obtained from:

DAVID C. COOK PUBLISHING CO.
850 NORTH GROVE AVENUE
ELGIN, IL 60120

or:

LAY ACTION MINISTRY PROGRAM, INC.
7200 E. DRY CREEK ROAD, SUITE D-202
ENGLEWOOD, CO 80112

303
730-8340 - Fax
800-707-5267

1

A WORD TO
BE EXPERIENCED

In his penetrating book, *Growing Strong in the Seasons of Life*, Pastor Chuck Swindoll tells about a former professional football coach considered the greatest of his era:

The late football strategist, Vince Lombardi, was a fanatic about fundamentals. Those who played under his leadership often spoke of his intensity, his drive, his endless enthusiasm for the guts of the game. Time and again he would come back to the basic techniques of blocking and tackling. On one occasion his team, the Green Bay Packers, lost to an inferior squad. It was bad enough to lose . . . but to lose to that team was absolutely inexcusable. Coach Lombardi called a practice the very next morning. The men sat silently, looking more like whipped puppies than a team of champions. They had no idea what to expect from the man they feared the most. Gritting his teeth and staring holes through one athlete after another, Lombardi began: "OK, we go back to the basics this morning . . ." Holding a football high enough for all to see, he continued to yell: ". . . Gentlemen, this is a football!" (From Growing Strong in the Seasons of Life, © 1983 by C. R. Swindoll, Multnomah Press: Portland, OR. Used by permission.)

Salvation Needed

Whether the setting is a football field or the broader arena of the Christian life, mastery of the basics is essential to success. *Welcome to the Church* covers a lot of the basics, and Lesson 1 puts the most basic subject of all under the microscope: salvation. It's important for all of Christ's team members to understand this term. More significantly, it's a word that must be experienced before one can be a part of His team!

The word salvation means "deliverance." It suggests that we're in some type of danger and need to be snatched away, to be brought to a place of safety. In the Old Testament, the concept of salvation often refers to deliverance of Israel from some enemy nation. When we apply the term to Christian experience, we have a different kind of deliverance in mind.

1. Why does every human being need deliverance, according to:

Jeremiah 17:9 *Sick on inside incurable*

Romans 3:10-12, 23 *all self-kings*

Mark 7:14-23 *Not environment, Not past, Heart*

> We were created with a capacity to know God and to have fellowship with Him (Gen. 2). But the first couple, Adam and Eve, decided to disobey God (Gen. 3). Their disobedience immediately cut them off from a relationship with God. This cut-off-from-God state was passed down through all mankind (Rom. 5:12).

2. Read I Peter 1:15, 16. What is there about God that makes it impossible for Him to have fellowship with marred independent human beings?

He is holy.

How frustrating! We have a natural bent to go our own way (called a "sinful nature"), so we're cut off from a relationship with a perfect God. This sin nature has far-reaching effects. It limits our ability to understand spiritual things. It damages our emotions to the extent that we can't fully trust them. Left unchecked, this sin nature also warps the conscience and blots out a

sense of right and wrong. This tendency toward inde-
pendence from God also weakens the will, limiting our
ability to do what we know is right.

3. Check Romans 5:12 and 6:23. What is the ultimate
consequence of sin? *Eph. 2:1*

Death - Separation from God

4. So far, you've briefly reviewed why salvation is
needed. How well do you remember the concepts? The
word "salvation" means:

To be rescued from danger.

5. Now, in just two or three sentences describe why
salvation is needed. Your explanation should reflect an
understanding of both the character of persons, and the
character of God.

_God wants to have fellowship
with us but we are sinful at
heart. That sin separates us from
a holy God. We are unable
to remedy the problem ourself._

6. Remember one reference that clearly shows humanity's need for salvation. The reference I have chosen is:

_Mk 7:14-23_

Salvation Provided

We need deliverance—and we're unable to deliver
ourselves. Sounds bleak so far, doesn't it? But wait.
God took the initiative and dealt a knockout punch to
the sin problem. Look up the passages that follow and
review what God did for humankind, and how He
provided what the Bible calls salvation. After each of
the following references, summarize its truth in your
own words. Try to find something distinctive in each
passage about God's provision of salvation.

Romans 5:6-11 _We were unable to save ourselves + God saved us when we were His enemies._

I John 4:9, 10 _God loves us so much that He gave His Son for us._

Ephesians 2:8, 9 _We cannot earn salvation we accept it by faith. God gives it as a gift._

Isaiah 53:4-6 _God punished Christ for our sins._

II Corinthians 5:21 _Christ became sin for us — We received His righteousness._

1. Which of the above passages speaks most clearly to you of God's provision of salvation? Explain. _+ indeed Rom 5:6-11 talks about our inability_

2. The verse I would like to share with someone needing salvation is _Rom 5:8_ . Memorize this verse! (Suggestion: Use the back of a business card to write out this verse and keep it in a shirt pocket or other handy location. Review it at least two times daily during the next week.)

3. What theological terms from the above passages would you like to understand better?

Seconds before taking His last breath on the cross, Jesus cried out, "It is finished" (Jn. 19:30). The same

10

word translated "finished" was found on a bill of debt dating back to the first century. The debt owed had been paid. This Greek word (meaning "paid in full") was boldly printed across the piece of paper, which then served as a receipt. Jesus was saying that the debt of sin has been "paid in full." What a relief! What a Savior!

Salvation Received

Though Jesus took the penalty for sin that each of us should have to pay, does that mean everyone is automatically saved? Of course not. *Each individual needs to turn to God.* God doesn't force salvation on anyone. He could have created a planet full of robots, programmed to blurt out, "We love You, God!" "We love You, God!" scores of times each day. But He didn't.

To be sure, salvation is a gift from God (Eph. 2:8, 9). It isn't something we work for. Yet what is involved in accepting His offer of salvation? Read the following verses and describe this experience: John 1:11, 12; Romans 10:9, 10; Revelation 3:20.

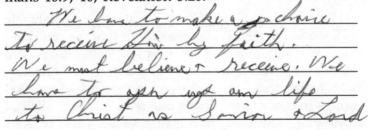

We have to make a choice to receive Him by faith. We must believe & receive. We have to open up our life to Christ as Savior & Lord

Have you responded to Jesus Christ in this way? Think again about your own salvation experience. You may have opportunity to share it in the group session. If you don't have anything to share, has God prepared your heart to receive Christ right now?

Select one verse showing how to receive salvation. Write out this verse on a small card. Commit it to memory for the next group meeting.

Salvation's Purpose

When Jesus Christ invades our lives, He has a two-fold purpose in mind. First, He restores our fellowship with God the Father, then He wants to deliver us from the control of sin (I Jn. 1:8-10).

Second . . . ah, here's where you get involved again! Instead of my telling you, find out for yourself. After each of the following references, jot down one or more phrases (directly from the Biblical text) which describe a second and different purpose of salvation. Though terms in the three passages will differ, the various phrases should point to a single purpose.

II Corinthians 5:17-20 _We are ambassadors to others_

Ephesians 2:8-10 _Created unto good works_

I Peter 2:9 _Declare His praises_

How exciting! God's gift of salvation is too valuable to keep to ourselves. He saves us so that we can share His love and message of salvation with others. No matter what vocation we're engaged in, we're ministers who have a message to share with persons whom God brings into our lives. That's one reason for the skeletal review of "salvation" in this first lesson. Most persons who complete this assignment already know Christ personally. But in order to fulfill this second broad purpose of salvation, we must be familiar enough with the truths and related Scriptures to share them with another person when God provides the opportunity. Unfortunately, research indicates that only a small percentage of Christians know how to use their Bibles to lead another person to faith in Jesus Christ. We want you—and others taking this course—to be a part of this minority!

Right now, think of one non-Christian person for whom you're concerned. Begin praying for his or her salvation today. Ask God to give you an opportunity, and the courage, to share what you've learned in this lesson with that individual.

The name of this non-Christian is:

_____

I can start improving my relationship with this person—with the ultimate goal of verbally sharing God's plan of salvation—in the following specific ways:

_____

_____

_____

_____

In addition to having a handle on Scripture, another factor that motivates us to share with non-Christians is seeing concrete changes Jesus is making in our behavior and value systems.

Once, in a well-to-do restaurant, someone accidently spilled ink onto an expensive handkerchief. An artist who sat at a nearby table saw the mess. He borrowed the handkerchief and sketched a beautiful picture on the marred cloth. He used the blotch of ink as part of the scenery. Similarly, when we experience salvation, God takes our messes and mistakes and begins the lifelong process of making something beautiful out of our lives.

In each of us, there are probably some "messes" still to be transformed by the Lord. Yet if we've come to Christ, He has begun a process of change in our lives. Perhaps you can already identify at least one area of your life where He has launched a beautifying process. If so, try to describe this change in a brief paragraph below.

_____

_____

_____

_____

_____

_____

_____

_____

_____

As God provides the opportunity for you to share with a non-Christian, convey *personal* ways you experience His benefits, as well as the Biblical truth reviewed earlier. Just as God did when He sent Jesus to earth, when you send someone the message of salvation, *wrap it in a person!* Keep in mind that people aren't interested in what we've done for God—but they may listen to what God has done for us!

2

SURE
THING!

Whether the setting is the physical realm or the spiritual, birth is only the beginning! If you've come to Christ recently, you're in the infant or toddler stage of a new life. That's certainly exciting! But as a young child quickly discovers, *the growth process has its ups and downs.*

New Christians sometimes stumble because of their doubts about personal salvation, or a pervasive sense of insecurity about their relationship to the Lord. If they don't respond Biblically to these fears and doubts, spiritual growth will be stunted.

That's why Lesson 2 tackles these questions: What causes us to doubt our conversion and the Lord's love for us? How can we be *sure* of the forgiveness of our sins and right standing with God—or can we? What are some facts about "life after rebirth" that can stabilize our daily walk with God?

Even if a lack of assurance doesn't badger you, it does pester a lot of people whom God brings into your life. What you learn in this lesson can enhance your capacity to minister to those persons.

Causes of Doubt

Let's survey four prominent reasons for spiritual insecurity in the life of a believer. These reasons aren't mutually exclusive—they may overlap at some points.

But for the sake of organization, let's probe them separately. Ready?

Reason #1: Depending Excessively on Feelings

Sometimes, when a person comes to Christ, it is an emotionally charged experience. But ecstatic feelings don't last forever, and God never intended that feelings control our behavior or our daily walk with Him.

Let's face it: not even spiritual giants sit on a "spiritual cloud 9" all the time. Tomorrow, if you don't feel close to the Lord, does that mean your conversion experience was phony and really didn't happen? Of course not! If you don't feel that God still loves you after you've failed, does that mean He has actually cast you out of His family? No!

Let's rivet three "F's" of the Christian life deeply into our consciousness. The first "F" is fact. The second "F" is faith. The third "F" is feeling. Your membership in God's family is rooted in the historical facts: Jesus came to earth, died on a cross as the perfect substitute for sinful humanity, then rose from the dead. When you became a Christian, you based your faith on those facts. You exercised your will, and in response to the wooing of God's Spirit, you asked Jesus to enter your life. By admitting your need of a Savior and putting faith in His work on the cross, you were born into God's family (Jn. 1:12). Your faith personalized the facts. Positive feelings are often the initial result of putting faith in the facts. But as we've already discussed, those feelings are fickle. The basis for our assurance of salvation is never our feelings; rather, it is the facts to which we've responded with faith.

Now, let's review:

1. Feelings can't be the basis of our assurance because:

feelings change

2. The three "F's" you read about should always be kept in proper order. If you were arranging them in a logical sequence, which would you put:

First _____ *Fact* _____

Second _____ *Faith* _____

Third _____ *Feelings* _____

A train diagram showing three cars (the engine, a passenger car, and a caboose) summarizes the relationship among the three "F's." Based on your understanding of the three "F's," label each car with one of the "F's." Which represents the engine, essential for the train's operation? Which represents the car that carries the passengers? Which is symbolized by the caboose, which tags along at the end?

Reason #2: Not Knowing God's Promises

Knowing the truths of God's Word doesn't automatically change us. We must also apply them. On the other hand, doubts will enter a blank mind more readily than a mind filled with the knowledge of God's Word. The Bible contains truths that, if known, can boost our trust level and increase our confidence as Christians. The more we know about God and how He relates to us as His children, the more ammunition we have to battle satanic lies and doubts (read Eph. 6:10-18).

Imagine that yesterday you committed what you would consider a "big" sin. You felt genuine sorrow, so you promptly confessed it to the Lord and claimed His forgiveness. Yet a day later, that sin still haunts you;

you don't feel forgiven; you feel insecure in God's presence, as if He is holding it against you.

What do the following verses contribute to the solution of the hypothetical problem above?

Proverbs 28:13 _Confession brings mercy_

Isaiah 55:7 _Mercy + pardon to a repentant_

I John 2:1, 2 _Jesus intercedes for us_

I John 1:9 _Confession = forgiveness_

God's Word is always more reliable than our feelings!

Reason #3: Misunderstanding Our Status Before God

This cause of doubt, though treated as a separate point, also shows how a grasp of the Bible combats lack of assurance. Do we occasionally "put ourselves on the cross," and try to improve on, or add to, the sacrifice Jesus made for our sins?

That's an unusual way of putting it, but I'm convinced that it's something we do. We mope around and carry the emotional burden of sins we've already confessed. Subconsciously, we feel we must inflict pain upon ourselves to prove to God that we're sorry for our sins. And we "put ourselves on the cross" when we delay prayer after we've blown it spiritually because we're afraid He won't accept us.

How crucial it is to grasp and internalize our status of complete forgiveness and acceptance before God! It must become entrenched deep within our self-image. Misunderstanding at this point creates spiritual insecurity. It's a top-shelf priority to sink our teeth into Scriptures that can increase our confidence before God.

3. Look at Romans 5:1, 2. Specific words and/or phrases that describe a Christian's status before the Heavenly Father include:

Justified + at peace w/ God

18

4. Now turn over a few pages and examine Romans 8:1, 31-39. Jot down every word and/or phrase that describes a Christian's standing before God, or God's attitude toward all who have received Christ.

No condemnation — nothing can separate us.

Reason #4: Failing in Our Daily Walk with God

It's possible to doubt the reality of our conversion because we sin. After all, Scripture makes it plain that evidences of new life will emerge in the life of a convert. If no changes occur, we reason, perhaps it means that Jesus never really entered our lives. Yet some changes will happen very gradually, over a period of time. Maturity doesn't occur with push-button ease.

Have you ever seen somone wearing a button with these letters printed on it: PBPGIFWMY? The letters stand for, "Please Be Patient. God Isn't Finished With Me Yet." The button stems from Philippians 1:6: "Being confident of this, that He who began a good work in you will carry it on to completion until the day of Christ Jesus."

Sinning after conversion shows that salvation doesn't completely wipe out our sinful nature (I Jn. 1:8). God's Spirit has moved in, and we have a new power to obey the Lord and resist temptation. But the "old" and "new" nature coexist, each vying for control. When we fail the Lord, instead of questioning the reality of our salvation, we can follow the apostle John's advice to "confess our sins" and claim the promise that "He is faithful and just and will forgive us our sins and purify us from all unrighteousness" (I Jn. 1:9).

5. Read Philippians 1:6 again, and paraphrase it (put it in your own words without changing its meaning):

_____

_____

_____

_____

A Look at Life-Style

Before leaving this lesson, it's important to examine what I John says about assurance of salvation. John wrote this letter so his readers would know that they have eternal life (5:13). Woven throughout the five chapters are evidences that readers can use to evaluate their relationship with Jesus Christ. If one is a Christian, a new life will begin to express itself. The evidences of salvation that John lists are marks of newness that differentiate Christians from non-Christians.

Mull over the following verses. Following each set, jot down the evidence of salvation that John cites. (Careful, though. Remember that no one exhibits each mark of newness to a perfect degree. These evidences grow in us as we grow in Christ. The point is this: can we see qualitative differences in our lives now, compared to our lives before Christ?)

Basis #1: I John 2:3-6 (see also Jn. 14:21; 15:10).

_____

Basis #2: I John 2:19, 24, 25 (see also II Tim. 4:1; Heb. 3:12; 10:24, 25).

_____

Basis #3: I John 2:29; 3:10 (see also I Cor. 15:34; Eph. 6:14).

_____

Basis #4: I John 2:9-11; 3:14; 4:7, 8 (see also Jn. 13:35).

_____

Basis #5: I John 3:24; 4:13 (see also Rom. 8:9).

_____

Basis #6: I John 5:4, 5 (see also Rom. 8:35-37; Rev. 2:7).

_____

Basis #7: I John 5:10-13 (see also Rom. 10:9, 10).

_____

Formulate a statement that expresses the overall impact of these seven bases for assurance.

_____

_____

_____

_____

List one or more areas where you see the need for greater consistency in your Christian life. Make this a matter of special prayer before the Lord.

_____

_____

Buried Treasure

Pick out one of the Bible references on assurance in Lesson 2 to memorize. Write it on a small card and review it daily between now and the next meeting of your study group.

KNOWING GOD THE FATHER

How do other people get to know you? How do they find out your hobbies, your favorite foods, your most cherished memories? How do they become aware of your innermost joys and burdens? Your goals for the future?

Perhaps they uncover a few facts about you from your friends and relatives. Most of their information, though, comes directly from you. They can't get to know you well unless you choose to reveal information about yourself. Your *revelation* of self is the key to others' knowledge of you. The more you're willing to reveal, the more intimately others can know you.

"Revelation" is an important word for Christians. All religions except Christianity began with a human attempt to discover or to explain God. But Christianity began with God's attempt to reach humanity! God took the initiative. He decided to create humankind and to reveal Himself to us for the purpose of enjoying an ongoing relationship with us. Primarily through the Bible and the person of Jesus Christ, God has revealed His nature, His plans, and His will for Creation. Without His deliberate revelation, we couldn't know what God is like, what He has done in history, or what He will do in the future.

In this lesson, you will take a closer look at what God has revealed about Himself in the Bible. Your primary focus will be on God's character qualities, and on practical implications for the nitty-gritty of your life. In just one study it's impossible to plumb the depths of God's character. But unless I miss my guess, when you finish this assignment you'll know Him better than you do now.

Character Sketch

God the Father has both supernatural traits (those not available to humans) and human traits (those which can describe humans as well as God). Even when we ascribe human traits to Him, though, let's remember that He has those capacities in a perfect and complete sense. Scripture depicts God as a Person who can think, create, make decisions, feel, and communicate. He isn't the mysterious, impersonal "Force" of *Star Wars* fame.

Open your Bible to the following passages. Jot down what you learn about God the Father:

Passage / Characteristic / What is said about God?

Psalms 90:1, 2; 93:2 _Eternity, Creator, God is the source of our life. It is in Him that we have life._

Psalms 86:15; 103:8, 9 _Gracious, Merciful God is compassionate with me._

Psalm 119:68 _Goodness God is a good God. What He does with me will be good._

Psalm 139:1-4 _Omniscient God has personal knowledge of me and my life._

Psalm 139:7-10; Jeremiah 23:24 _Omnipresence God is everywhere I am. God is always w/me._

Psalm 147:5 _Omnipotent God who is w/me is all powerful_

Leviticus 20:26; Isaiah 6:1-6 _Holy God is completely_ _different from me in His holiness. Worship_ _humility_

Jeremiah 32:17 _Nothing too hard for_ _God._

John 4:24 _God does not have a body. When_ _you worship God you come to a spirit person._

Titus 1:2 _God will not lie to us._ _God's plans will be accomplished_

James 1:17 _All good things come from God._ _That will never change._

Glance over your completed work. Those attributes aren't just cold, sterile theology. They describe a dynamic, active God who's involved in your life on a daily basis. In the space provided below, list three of the attributes (from your responses above) that God has expressed in relationship to you during the past month. Briefly describe how you experienced or benefited from each quality.

1. _Nothing too hard — God enabled me to_ _deeply touch my wife's heart w/ love._

2. _Truth — I sought God's counsel_ _from the story of Gideon._

3. _____

So What?

What difference should knowing these things about God make in our daily lives? That's a healthy question!

24

You aren't interested in a Ripley's "Believe It Or Not" record for the number of Biblical facts crammed into one head. Bible knowledge should always flow from the head, and irrigate the heart.

How is it helpful to know that God is all knowing? Changeless? All powerful? Truthful? You guessed it. Rather than provide a list of neatly packaged answers, it's time for you to wrestle with that question, and roll a few "so whats" around in your mind.

To the right of each characteristic, write down one or more applications. I've provided an example to get you started.

God Is . . . Therefore . . .

All knowing: *I'M FREE TO BE MORE HONEST IN MY PRAYERS. WHY TRY TO KEEP FROM GOD MY SECRET SINS, MY HIDDEN HURTS AND DESIRES?*

All powerful: *In following God, I'm never trapped - like the Israelites at the Red Sea. God can do anything.*

Holy: *I'm not free to do whatever I want. My life must reflect God's holiness.*

Compassionate or loving: *There is always hope w/regard to sin. God will forgive, God will make a way.*

Truthful: *I have a counsellor available to me.*

25

Changeless: _This world is in constant flux. God is not. He provides real stability._

Wise, infinite in understanding: _God knows me completely. He is in control of my life. Confidence & security_

Omnipresent (everywhere at once): _He is a friend (parakaleo) who sticks close. Always accessible._

Most individual and corporate praise to God is in response to things He has done. That's valid. Yet God merits praise and honor just for who He is. Right now, write a thank-You note to God the Father. Pick out one of the attributes from this lesson that means a lot to you personally. Tell Him why you appreciate that aspect of His nature.

Dear God

I thank you that I can count on you to be the same God you always have been. You are a strong anchor in the storms of my life. You won't be taken from me and you won't leave me. You are most worthy of all honor, worship and Love.

4

KNOWING
JESUS CHRIST

Have you read that anonymous piece titled "One Solitary Life"? Here it is:

He was born in an obscure village, the child of a peasant woman.

He grew up in still another village, where he worked in a carpenter's shop till he was thirty. Then for three years he was an itinerant preacher.

He never wrote a book. He never held an office. He never had a family or owned a house. He didn't go to college. He never visited a big city. He never traveled two hundred miles from the place where he was born. He did none of the things one usually associates with greatness.

He had no credentials but himself.

He was only thirty-three when the tide of public opinion turned against him. His friends ran away. He was turned over to his enemies and went through the mockery of a trial. He was nailed to a cross between two thieves. While he was dying, his executioners gambled for his clothing, the only property he had on earth. When he was dead he was laid in a borrowed grave through the pity of a friend.

Nineteen centuries have come and gone, and today he is the central figure of the human race and the leader of mankind's progress. All the armies that ever marched, all the navies that ever sailed, all the parliaments that ever sat, all the kings that ever reigned, put together, have not affected the life of man on this earth as much as that one *solitary life.*

Who Is Jesus?

Why did Jesus Christ leave such an impact on human history? What makes Him different from other founders of religious movements, such as Buddha or Mohammed? Why do we Christians insist that He's the *only* way to God and to eternal life?

Chances are, we can answer these questions right now well enough to earn a passing score. However, we want a more thorough understanding of Jesus Christ's life and work. One lesson can't cover everything we need to know about Him. But these assignments provide a starting place. During the next hour or so, you'll become more familiar with who He is, why He came, and what He's doing in the world. Before you proceed, ask the Lord to meet you personally through the Scriptures you read. You want knowledge about Him to increase your intimacy with Him.

Paul's Portrait of Christ

The first two chapters of Colossians are teeming with doctrinal teachings about Jesus Christ. Paul wanted to impress the Colossians, who were threatened by false teachings, with the centrality that Jesus must have in the thought and behavior of a Christian. Let's zero in on Colossians 1:13-20, and let it serve as a launching pad for our study. After reading these verses a couple times, tackle the following questions:

1. What labels, or titles does Paul give to Christ? (Pick out words and/or phrases directly from the text.)

"image of invisible God"; "Firstborn over all creation";
Head of body

2. Specifically, what actions, or works of Jesus does Paul mention?

v.15 Revelation   v.16 Creator   v.17 Sustainer
Supremacy   Reconciler   Makes Peace

28

3. Now mull over the answers you wrote to the two previous questions. What major purposes for the earthly life and ministry of Christ can you glean from Colossians 1:13-20? (Try to find at least two.)

Reveal God to man.
Reconcile Man to God.
Establish His supremacy

4. A part of this passage that I'm not sure I understand clearly is:

5. One new truth I uncovered about Jesus Christ is:

6. The insight about Jesus Christ that is most meaningful to me right now is:

That He holds all things together.

because:

Life seems very unstable

Jesus—God Himself!

Undoubtedly, one of the things you gleaned from Colossians 1:13-20 was a reference to Jesus' _deity_. Paul called Him "the image of the invisible God" (Col. 1:15), and God's beloved Son (Col. 1:13). If Jesus Christ had been _only_ a man—no matter how great a leader He was—He wouldn't deserve our allegiance and worship. He was fully man, _and_ fully God!

It's helpful to remind ourselves of the specific evidences of Jesus' deity. This information can reassure us and deepen our faith in Christ. It can equip us to share with people who have doubts about who Jesus really is. Many people whom we meet aren't convinced that Jesus was God in human flesh. Many of them don't even believe that the Bible portrays Jesus as deity!

Read each set of Scripture references below, then jot down the evidence of Jesus' deity that is given. Some references may say specific things about Christ. Others may show Christ in action, doing something that only God Himself could do. The entry for the first set of references is an example.

Scripture: Evidence Identified:

Scripture	Evidence Identified
Colossians 1:16,17 John 1:1-3, 14 John 8:58	THESE VERSES REFER TO JESUS' PRE-EXISTENCE. HE EXISTED BEFORE HE WAS BORN IN HUMAN FORM.
John 5:18; 10:30 John 19:7 Matthew 26:63-66	He claimed to be the real Son of God making Himself of the same nature as God. when accused of Claiming to be equal w/ Father He did not deny.
Mark 2:5-11 (focus on vss. 5-7)	He claimed + exercised the authority + power to forgive sins. Even those not against Him. Only God can forgive sins.
Mark 1:23-27 Mark 5:1-13 (focus on vss. 6, 7)	He had the power and authority to order evil spirits and have them immediately obey.
John 6:1-14 John 9:1-7 John 11:38-45	Jesus had the power to alter nature. Create Food, sight, life

30

I John 3:5
I Peter 2:21, 22

He never sinned!

Romans 1:4
Acts 13:32-37

Jesus rose from the dead. Never to die again, as predicted in the O.T.

Which evidence of Jesus' deity impresses you most? Why?

Claiming to be equal w/ God
Not sinning   Resurrection

Jesus' Number-One Accomplishment

In Colossians 1:13-20, you saw references to Jesus' *work* on our behalf. You were even asked to glean from the passage at least two broad purposes for His coming to earth. When your group meets again, your leader will probe the Colossian passage with you, and you'll discuss specific answers to the questions in the "Paul's Portrait of Christ" section of this lesson.

However, it's essential to emphasize the *primary reason* for Jesus' coming to earth. You examined this reason in the lessons on salvation and assurance of salvation. Briefly, look at Romans 5:6-11. In your own words, summarize why Jesus came.

We didn't want anything to do w/ God and we couldn't secure a relationship w/ Him, if we wanted to. Jesus came to make the way.

The content and structure of the four Gospels also reveal that *why Jesus came* was the most significant element of His life. Jesus lived on earth approximately 1700 weeks. In Mark's Gospel, chapters 1-10 cover Jesus' first 1699 weeks, and chapters 11-16 cover His last

31

week! This proportion shows that Mark wanted to emphasize Jesus' *death for our sins*. "For even the Son of Man did not come to be served, but to serve, and to give his life a ransom for many" (Mark 10:45).

Just think of it—*you and I* are the reason He came to earth! And it's our privilege to inform others of what Jesus accomplished, so they can also reap the benefits.

Current Job Description

Of course, Jesus' death would have accomplished nothing if He hadn't risen from the grave, and ascended into Heaven. But what became of the Son of God after He abandoned His life in the flesh? He didn't retire to some plush lake resort in Heaven, leaving all the work to God the Father and the Holy Spirit. No, He is still active on our behalf.

The following passages mention some of the roles He now fills. Study each set of passages, and jot down the present ministry of Christ referred to.

John 14:1-3 _Preparing heaven; Returning to get us._

Romans 8:34; Hebrews 4:14; 7:23-25 _Intercedes for us helps us_

Original Christmas Card

Here is a good way to close this sketch of Jesus' life and ministry: in the space provided below, write and design a unique Christmas card. This is a way of personalizing a study on Jesus' life. Your words could consist of a brief poem, or just one sentence with an appropriate Scripture verse. Here are a couple of ideas to serve as catalysts for your thoughts:

- The face of the card consists of a series of huge question marks. Printed below the question marks is: HOW DO I KNOW GOD LOVES ME? Open the card, and you see: . . . . BECAUSE HE CARED ENOUGH

TO SEND THE VERY BEST! (Then Jn. 3:16 is printed in smaller letters.)

- Using the same format, the cover reads: WHEN GOD HAD A GIFT TO SEND . . . The inside says: . . . HE WRAPPED IT IN A PERSON—JESUS CHRIST! (Then Gal. 4:4, 5 is printed in smaller letters.)

Remember—these are just samples. Come up with your own greeting as a love response to Jesus Christ.

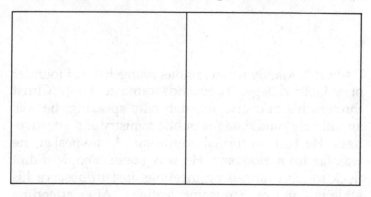

Fellowship Idea

No matter what time of year it is, use your original Christmas card greeting as a means of initiating an enjoyable evening with a few friends in your church. Think of singles or couples outside your Bible study group whom you'd like to know better. Find a blank card that you can design and write on. You can slip a note in the card, inviting them over for dinner, or for a dessert after a Sunday evening church service. You can also explain briefly why you're using a Christmas greeting, so they'll know it's an outgrowth of a Bible study on the life of Jesus.

Jesus is the basis for our fellowship with other Christians. Without a common allegiance to Him, the intimacy of Christian friendship is impossible.

5

KNOWING THE HOLY SPIRIT

Dwight L. Moody was a famous evangelist and founder of a Bible college. Thousands came to know Christ through his ministry. Yet, naturally speaking, he was an unlikely candidate for public ministry and effectiveness. He had no formal education. As a speaker, he was far from eloquent. He was obese. People didn't flock to his evangelistic meetings just to observe his athletic build or handsome features. After attending one of his campaigns, a secular writer observed, "I can find no natural explanation for Mr. Moody's success." When Moody read the column from which that quote was taken, he said, "That's because there is no *natural* explanation."

The explanation for D. L. Moody's impact on history is a *supernatural* one. When he was visiting England early in his ministry, he heard Henry Varley say, "The world has yet to see what God can do with a man who is fully and wholly consecrated to the Holy Spirit."

Moody thought to himself, "He said 'a man.' He meant any man. He didn't say he had to be brilliant or educated or anything else. Just a man. Well, by the Holy Spirit in me, I will be that man."

The same Holy Spirit who changed and used D. L. Moody, can change and use any man or woman who is willing. Let's get better acquainted with Him as a Person. The clearer we grasp what the Bible says about the Holy Spirit, the more responsive we can be to Him.

Permanent Address

The one God in whom Christians believe exists in *three persons:* God the Father, God the Son, and God the Holy Spirit. This hard-to-grasp but important teaching about God is called the *Trinity*. (The fact that there is only one God is called His *unity*. The mind-stretching truth that He exists in three persons is called His "tri-unity," or "trinity.")

This perspective is significant because we must view the Holy Spirit as a *Person* who has all the qualities and characteristcs of God. He isn't some impersonal force, or some sort of optional benefit of Christian experience.

Read Romans 8:9. Pay close attention to the last half of the verse. Put a **T** by the statement that is true, and an **F** by the statement that is false:

_F_ The Holy Spirit (called the "Spirit of Christ" in Romans 8:9) is a special blessing, given to some Christians, but not to all Christians.

_T_ A person cannot be a Christian unless he or she has the Holy Spirit. All Christians have the benefit of the Spirit's presence in their lives.

Next, examine I Corinthians 3:16, 17 and 6:19, 20. What is the "permanent address," or dwelling place, of the Holy Spirit?

The heart of the believer.

One personal application of the fact that the Holy Spirit resides within me is:

I have God's power at hand.

Jesus' Teaching on the Holy Spirit

In what is called The Upper Room Discourse, recorded in John 13—16, Jesus introduced the disciples to the

Holy Spirit. Jesus' crucifixion was just around the corner. He wanted to prepare the disciples for His impending death, and ascension to Heaven. To encourage them, He promised that He wouldn't leave them alone. God the Father would send another Person—the Holy Spirit—to enable them. Jesus' promise was fulfilled on what has been called the Day of Pentecost, recorded in Acts 2. That's when the Holy Spirit came to indwell Christians. The event launched the first local Christian church in Jerusalem, and His Church has been expanding ever since.

1. Let's take a closer look at what Jesus taught concerning the Holy Spirit. Glance at John 14:16-18, 26; and John 16:7-15. How did Jesus describe the Holy Spirit? Specifically, what titles did He use? *Rev 22:18ff*

Another Counsellor (Parakletos); Spirit of truth; unacceptable to world; Holy Spirit Teacher, Reminder; Convictor; Truth Guide; Prophecy; Revealer of Jesus

One of the terms Jesus used to describe the Spirit is translated "Helper" or "Comforter." Literally, the word means "One who comes alongside to help." The verb form of this term means "to encourage."

To feel the impact of this definition, think of a jumper cable. In one car, the battery is too weak to run the car. A car with a good battery pulls alongside. The jumper cable connects the powerful battery to the weak battery. Then power flows through the jumper cable, and the weaker battery is infused with new strength and potential. Similarly, the Holy Spirit continually comes alongside of us to lend encouragement and the strength to press on when our spiritual batteries seem weak. You'll discover more about His specific ministries later. But even now, you can use this analogy to reflect on the Spirit's work in your behalf.

2. Write a few sentences that describe one specific way

36

He has "come alongside" you and ministered to you in the past.

Helped me talk to Adam.
When Adam needed me and
I didn't know it.

3. Now shift your focus to the upcoming weeks. Think about ensuing events, decisions you'll have to make, etc. Jot down one or two situations you'll face in which you'll need the Holy Spirit to come alongside and help in a special way.

Preaching series

Moving boys closer to God.

4. Let's move the spotlight back to Jesus' discourse. Look at John 14:26 and 16:13-15. What is the Holy Spirit's role in relation to Jesus Christ?

Represent Christ + teach the
disciples (+ us) about Him.

5. Mull over the same verses again, and add I Corinthians 2:7-11 to your study. What is the Holy Spirit's role in relation to the truth of God? (Include the truth which came through Christ's words, and the whole truth of God which we now have in the Bible.)

To open our understanding
to Gods truth.

6. John 16:7-11 emphasizes the Holy Spirit's function in relation to the world, or in the lives of unbelievers. If we really believe that conviction of sin is a supernatural work of the Holy Spirit, how can we apply this fact to

our witnessing efforts and to our relationships with
non-Christians?

We need to pray for the lost
that the H.S. would open their minds
+ hearts to the truth + bring
conviction.

An Active Person

Jesus referred to some of the Holy Spirit's ministries.
The following passages add to the list of things He has
done, or is doing, in our lives. Briefly list the work or
activity described in each passage.

I Corinthians 12:4-11 _gives gifts to_
enable ministry through
the Body

Romans 8:26, 27 _He prays for us_
according to God's will.

Acts 1:8 _gives power for witness_

Romans 8:15-17 _leads us;_
special privilege of sonship; Assures us,

Filled with the Holy Spirit

Though the Holy Spirit lives in every Christian, not
every Christian is "filled with the Spirit," or "walking"
in the Spirit. Many people are confused about what is
meant by the "filling of the Holy Spirit." And to be
honest, there are Christ-honoring groups who disagree
on the matter. We don't want to oversimplify the issue,
but what the Bible means by the fullness of the Holy
Spirit isn't as mysterious and complex as some make it
seem.

In his book, _Know What and Why You Believe_ (Victor
Books), the late Paul Little helps clarify the Biblical
teaching on the matter. Read this excerpt carefully:

The filling of the Spirit is an experience to be repeated as necessary in the life of each believer. We are, literally, to "keep on being filled" (Eph. 5:18).

The Holy Spirit is not a substance, but a Person. The fullness of the Spirit is not a matter of our receiving more of Him. Rather, it is a matter of relationship. To be filled with the Spirit means we allow Him to occupy, guide, and control every area of our lives. His power can then work through us, making us effectively fruitful for God and flooding our hearts with His joy. This filling applies not only to our outward acts but to our inner thoughts and motives. When we are filled with the Spirit, all we are and have is subject to His control. *Bear Fruit*

The test as to whether or not you are filled with the Spirit is not, "Have you received an external sign or been given a particular gift of the Spirit?" Rather, "Have you given yourself wholly and without reservation to God?" (Rom. 12:1). Are you genuinely willing that He should control, absolutely and entirely, your life? Many believers come to a point of utter frustration in their service for the Lord simply because they fail to realize the need to be filled with the Spirit if they are to act in God's power. Just as we cannot save ourselves apart from the work of the Holy Spirit, neither can we live the life of victory or serve the Lord effectively without the Spirit. When we learn to trust Him fully, allowing Him to work through us, we are freed from the frustration of trying to accomplish spiritual and eternal results solely through our human ability—or, more properly, inability.

It is the Holy Spirit who delivers us from the power of sin. "For the law of the Spirit of life in Christ Jesus has made me free from the law of sin and death" (Rom. 8:2). The Holy Spirit changes the pattern of our life so that we can overcome sin. He does not make us sinless (I Jn. 1:8), but in Him we are able to start fulfilling the righteousness of the Law (Rom. 8:4). Such holy living is a work of the Spirit and a result of salvation; it is not in any way the basis for our being saved.

How well can you remember what you have read? Being filled with the Holy Spirit is not a matter of our _receiving_ more of Him; rather, it is a matter of _control_. The Holy Spirit is a _person_, not a substance. The test of whether or not a person is filled with the Holy Spirit is not _external sign or particular gift,_; rather, it is _given yourself w/o reservation to God_ How often does the filling of the Holy Spirit need to be repeated? _whenever I take back control from God._

A Christian leader named A. C. Dixon once said, "When we rely on organization, we get what organization can do. When we rely upon education, we get what education can do. When we rely on eloquence, we get what eloquence can do. But when we rely on the Holy Spirit, we get what *God* can do!"

Yes—God can work through organization, education, and gifts of eloquence. But Mr. Dixon's point is well taken: effectiveness in any Christian service endeavor requires the power of the Holy Spirit. Though God uses human instruments as teachers, administrators, witnesses, etc., it is *His* power that woos people to Him and changes their behavior.

Prayer Is the Key

Faithful prayer is our way of acknowledging the Spirit's centrality in ministry efforts. No matter how hard we work to evangelize, to teach, to make administrative decisions on church committees, we must continually ask for God's blessing. All ministry is a divine-human cooperation, ultimately dependent on supernatural activity for results.

Right now, think of your own ministry (your efforts to reach a non-Christian; teaching, hospitality, giving, discipling—you name it). Now think of a chunk of time *each day* when you could pray about this ministry in the months ahead. Even if it's only a three-minute prayer on the way to work, determine before God to make it a habit!

The best time of day for me to pray about the ministry God has given me is:

Immediately when I come home from work

Also, think of one individual or couple in your church whom you'd like to have pray for your ministry regularly. Jot down the name(s) here:

Within 24 hours, contact this individual or couple. Describe the ministry opportunity you're concerned about, and ask if he or she (or they) will pray for you at least a couple of times a week for the next three months. Be sure to contact your prayer partner(s) periodically to inform them of specific needs to pray about, or to share progress reports.

Yes, you'll encounter frustration, even opposition, in some of the things you do for the Lord. Don't be surprised by this, because Satan always tries to impede the progress of the Gospel. Be encouraged, though, by this closing truth about the Holy Spirit in relation to Satan: "The one who is in you is greater than the one who is in the world" (I Jn. 4:4b).

6

GOD'S PART...
AND MINE

A Christian chemistry professor at a large university once told his students, "Christianity is not a lecture. It is a laboratory science." He's right. Your faith is something to be practiced. It's validated by experimentation on a daily basis. And the laboratory is *life*—family relationships, job pressures, decisions that have to be made.

Time for Review

Before you delve into a new subject area, look back over your shoulder for a moment. What topical roads have you covered in this course so far?

First, you examined basic teachings on the salvation experience. That was followed by a lesson that gave Biblical assurances of salvation. The second lesson tried to encourage persons who wrestle with doubts and insecurities in their walk with the Lord. Lessons 3-5 gave you a closer look at the God who invaded your life, and transformed it, through salvation. Our one God exists in three Persons. And you devoted a single lesson to each Person: God the Father, God the Son (Jesus Christ), and God the Holy Spirit.

Now it's time to shift the focus. Lesson 6 launches a series of studies on "the walk and the warfare." You'll probe issues pertaining to a daily walk with the Lord. You'll consider the resources God provides for living as a Christian in a non-Christian world, and take a realistic look at the enemy who tries to impede your spiritual growth and block your ministry efforts.

This initial study in the new series provides an overarching perspective on Christian living. It's extremely important to develop a Biblical mindset before we can reap the full benefits from lessons on such subjects as Satan, prayer, the Bible, and the Church. Look at it this way—here is the "instructional manual" for using all the resources and equipment in our Christian life lab!

Where Does Discipline Fit In?

In a classic devotional book titled *The Disciplines of Life*, V. Raymond Edman, former president of Wheaton College, wrote: "Discipleship means discipline. Without discipline we are not disciples, even though we profess His name and pass for a follower of Jesus." Edman went on to describe how self-discipline is a prerequisite to successful Christian living and ministry.

We all nod in agreement with his statement. Too often, though, our *experience* of self-discipline isn't even close to what we *believe* about it. Why is this? Jot down some obstacles that often keep us from experiencing a mature level of discipline. Put another way, what keeps us from developing Christian discipline?

Busy lives; Laziness; idols; sinful indulgences; Anger toward God or others; Lack of faith.

If Dr. Edman was correct, then we must take seriously the development of discipline in our lives. And that begins by pondering hindrances to its development, and creating strategies to remove those hindrances.

For many people, one significant hindrance to the exercise of discipline is a misunderstanding about *how* we develop holiness of character—how we progress in our walk with the Lord. One extreme position is that spiritual growth has been left entirely up to us. By the exercise of sheer human willpower and determination alone, we attain greater and greater righteousness and live more effectively as Christians. In other words, the Lord has saved us, and now the ball is in our court. This view excessively elevates, or warps, the role of self-discipline. People who go this route tend to give up after a while. Repeated failure causes frustration, and they wonder why they can't measure up. Though it contains a measure of truth, this approach to Christian growth is unbalanced and unbiblical. It doesn't take seriously the limitations (caused by the sin nature) of our mere human willpower and self-effort. It forgets that even after we're saved, *inner transformation is still the work of God.* Just as we cannot receive salvation apart from His grace, we cannot take steps of Christian growth without His initiative and direct involvement in our lives.

On the other hand, some Christians swing the pendulum too far in the opposite direction. They acknowledge the insufficiency of human strivings, and conclude: "Since righteousness is always a result of God's grace, let's simply have faith and wait for Him to work in our lives. There is nothing we can do to facilitate the process."

This extreme position sounds spiritual enough, but it is also imbalanced and unbiblical. People with this mindset deemphasize the role of discipline. Some even shun spiritual discipline for fear of becoming legalistic. This attitude misinterprets "live by faith" (Gal. 2:20) to mean that God requires no human effort to live a holy life. It elevates God's provision for daily living at the expense of our clear-cut responsibility to obey Him.

Let's put the pendulum to rest somewhere in the middle. Though the issue is a profound one, perhaps the following excerpts from two well-known authors

44

can clarify it and put the role of self-discipline in a proper perspective. These statements should reveal the proper balance between God's part . . . and ours.

A farmer plows his field, sows the seed, and fertilizes and cultivates—all the while knowing that in the final analysis he is utterly dependent on forces outside of himself. He knows he cannot cause the seed to germinate, nor can he produce the rain and sunshine for growing and harvesting the crop. For a successful harvest, he is dependent on these things from God.

Yet the farmer knows that unless he diligently pursues his responsibilities to plow, plant, fertilize, and cultivate, he cannot expect a harvest at the end of the season. In a sense he is in a partnership with God, and he will reap its benefits only when he has fulfilled his own responsibilities.

Farming is a joint venture between God and the farmer. The farmer cannot do what God must do, and God will not do what the farmer should do.

We can say just as accurately that the pursuit of holiness is a joint venture between God and the Christian. No one can attain any degree of holiness without God's working in his life, but just as surely no one will attain it without effort on his own part. God has made it possible for us to walk in holiness. But He has given to us the responsibility of doing the walking; He does not do that for us.

We Christians greatly enjoy talking about the provision of God, how Christ defeated sin on the cross and gave us His Holy Spirit to empower us to victory over sin. But we do not as readily talk about our own responsibility to walk in holiness. Two primary reasons can be given for this.

First, we are simply reluctant to face up to our responsibility. We prefer to leave that to God. We pray for victory when we know we should be acting in obedience.

The second reason is that we do not understand the proper distinction between God's provision and our own responsibility for holiness. I struggled for a number of years with the question, "What am I to do myself, and what am I to rely on God to do?" Only as I came to see what the Bible teaches on

*this question, and then faced up to my own responsibility, did
I see any progress in the "pursuit of holiness."*

*The title for this book comes from the biblical command,
"Pursue holiness, for without holiness no one will see the
Lord." (Hebrews 12:14, author's paraphrase). The word pursue suggests two thoughts: first, that diligence and effort are
required; and second, that it is a lifelong task.*

—Jerry Bridges, *The Pursuit of Holiness*
(© 1978 by the Navigators. Used by permission of NavPress, Colorado Springs, CO. All rights reserved.)

In *Celebration of Discipline: The Path to Spiritual Growth,*
(Harper and Row) Richard Foster piggybacks on what
Bridges has said. Before you read the following excerpt
from his book be aware of what he means by the
"Spiritual Disciplines." He's referring to life-style pat-
terns which are central to experiential Christianity, such
as prayer, Bible study, service, and corporate worship.

*We do not need to be hung on the horns of the dilemma of
either human works or idleness. God has given us the Disciplines of the spiritual life as a means of receiving His grace.
The Disciplines allow us to place ourselves before God so that
He can transform us.*

*The apostle Paul said, "He who sows to his own flesh will
from the flesh reap corruption; but he who sows to the Spirit
will from the Spirit reap eternal life" (Gal. 6:8). A farmer is
helpless to grow grain; all he can do is to provide the right
conditions for the growing of grain. He puts the seed in the
ground where the natural forces take over and up comes the
grain. That is the way with the Spiritual Disciplines—they
are a way of sowing to the Spirit. The Disciplines are God's
way of getting us into the ground; they put us where He can
work within us and transform us. By themselves the Spiritual
Disciplines can do nothing; they can only get us to the place
where something can be done. They are God's means of grace.
The inner righteousness we seek is not something that is
poured on our heads. God has ordained the Disciplines of the
spiritual life as the means by which we are placed where He*

46

can bless us. In this regard it would be proper to speak of "the way of disciplined grace." It is "grace" because it is free; it is "disciplined" because there is something for us to do.

Let's Crystalize It

1. *Discipline* is an essential trait of a follower of Christ.

2. One hindrance to the exercise of *discipline* in a life is a misunderstanding regarding *how* we develop holiness, and make progress spiritually.

3. Two extreme positions regarding the relationship between God's part and our part in spiritual growth, both of which are imbalanced and inappropriate, could be summarized as follows. (Describe each approach in your own words.)

The position that overemphasizes our part:

God has saved us now it is our job to make us holy.

The position that deemphasizes our responsibility:

We are sinful + can do nothing helpful. Just get out of the way + let God.

4. The Bible verse that Bridges employed to validate his line of reasoning is *Heb 12:14* . (Read this verse again in several different translations.)

5. How does the farming analogy, employed by both Bridges and Foster, clarify the relationship between God's part and our part in daily Christian living?

If we don't do something (put seed in Ground) God can't grow it.

6. Richard Foster summarized what he perceives to be a Biblical position by calling it "the way of disciplined grace." It's "grace" because: *it is free*

It is "disciplined" because:

there is something for
_me to do_

Put simply, the proper application of discipline, to which Edman referred, constantly involves us in *choosing to use* the means of grace that God has made available. For instance, He works through His Word, but we may choose whether or not to study it. He works through prayer, but only when we choose to pray!

Implementing My Part

What Foster called "Spiritual Disciplines" or "means of grace" are merely the avenues through which God meets and empowers us. A few of the disciplines will be covered in future lessons, but for now, read each set of Scripture references and describe what they call us to do.

1. John 15:7 (note the first part of the verse); II Timothy 3:14-17.

I stay in Christ by staying
in the Word.

2. John 16:24; Colossians 4:2; Philippians 4:6, 7.

God to God regularly
in prayer asking for
things.

3. I Corinthans 12:12-27; Hebrews 10:24, 25.

God has put together
the body of Christ to
meet one anothers needs.

4. Which of the three disciplines, or courses of action, listed above, have you been implementing most successfully?

Body Life

5. Briefly describe one specific way God has met you, or graciously worked in your life, as a result of your action.

Emmaus small
group

You just verified from experience what was theoretically explained in the first few pages of this lesson. God deserves the credit for changes produced in your life, yet you first decided to tap into His power through times of Bible study, prayer, and involvement with other Christians.

6. Now mull over this question. Which of the three Scriptural means of growth do you least consistently practice?

Prayer Word

7. What changes in your schedule are necessary in order to regularly exercise this means of spiritual growth?

Spend time

8. Read the following Bible verses: Ephesians 3:20, 21; Philippians 1:6; 2:13; and 4:13. How could these verses encourage someone who is discouraged about his or her ability to change? (Also what is the relationship between the truth of these verses and your previous lesson on the Holy Spirit?)

God is more than able &
willing. The HS in me

Use It or Lose It

Are you aware that the Lord never instructs or comforts you solely for your own benefit? He constantly wants to use you as a channel through whom He can bless others.

Think about the helpful insights you're gleaning from this course. Over the next few weeks, be thinking of ways you can convey to others—particularly persons new in the faith—what you're learning. Whether or not you consider yourself a teacher in a formal sense, be open to the possibility of systematically leading others through this workbook. One way you could do this would be to lead another small group through this study, over a period of 13 weeks. If you feel a nudge from the Lord in this direction, consult with your pastor about the possibility.

Another way, much more informal, is to go through the workbook weekly with one other person or couple. A businessman could have a 7:00 a.m. breakfast appointment once a week to go over this material with a new Christian from the office as a means of discipling him. Or a married couple could meet one hour a week with one or two other couples and informally lead them through the material.

Ask the Lord to give you the names of one or more new Christians whom you could lead through this course. Ask your spouse and current group leader to pray with you about it. Just keep in mind that whomever you invite to go through the lessons with you will have to make a weekly commitment to fulfill the workbook asignment. If a door opens for this kind of ministry, see your current group leader for advice, and work through your leader to obtain extra copies of *Welcome to the Church*.

7

FOES OF
THE FAITH

Scouting the opponent is big business! You name the sport—all professional teams devote a hefty chunk of the budget to the salaries and travel expenses of their scouts.

For instance, if the New York Yankees baseball team is scheduled to play the Chicago White Sox in an important series, the team flies a scout to Chicago a week in advance. The scout watches the White Sox play another opponent. He notes the hitters in a slump, and those on a hot streak. If a White Sox outfielder has a weak arm, he scribbles in his notebook that a base runner can take an extra base on the guy. He sends a report back to New York, chock full of details about player capabilities and coaching strategies.

Why go to all the expense? Because *knowledge of the opponent is essential to competing successfully against him.*

Know Your Opponent!

There's a corollary between this facet of sports, and the Christian life. Knowing the characteristics and strategies of our foes enables us to defend ourselves against them. In this lesson, we'll scout the opponents who try to keep us from scoring spiritually. And we'll learn how to compete against these foes, and wind up in the win column after our daily battles.

Let's Backtrack for a Moment

In Lesson 6, you learned that you have the responsibility to exercise the means of growth that God has made available. Character transformation and fruit-bearing service is a *supernatural* work of God, yet He has chosen to meet and to empower you through the disciplines of Christian living, such as prayer, Bible study, and involvement in authentic fellowship. But you must choose whether or not to tap into God's resources for holiness and power.

This lesson stems naturally from Lesson 6. As you delve into it, you'll discover why disciplining yourself and walking consistently with the Lord is often such a struggle. There are forces competing against our desire to serve Jesus Christ. Our walk is sometimes a warfare. That's a fact of Christian living that we must face realistically.

Three Common Opponents of Every Christian

Three separate forces are actually warring against the Holy Spirit for control of our thoughts, decisions, and behavior. These forces work in tandem with one another in order to usurp Christ's authority over our lives.

1. To discover the first foe, sink your teeth into the following references: Galatians 5:16-21 and Mark 7:14-23. The first foe that dogs my feet as a Christian is:

My own evil heart

When you became a Christian, God's Spirit invaded your life. You now have a new capacity to obey the Lord and resist wrongdoing. On the other hand, salvation didn't completely blot out that deep-seated tendency to go your own way. Within you coexist two natures: the "old" and the "new," each vying for control. The first foe on the list is that "old" nature, which constantly tries to pull you down spiritually. In his book *The Pursuit of Holiness*, Jerry Bridges vividly illustrates the

52

internal tug-of-war between this sinful nature and your new nature in Christ.

In a particular nation, two competing factions were fighting for control of the country. Eventually, with the help of an outside army, one faction won the war and assumed control of the nation's government. But the losing side did not stop fighting. They simply changed their tactics to guerrilla warfare and continued to fight. In fact, they were so successful that the country supplying the outside help could not withdraw its troops.

So it is with the Christian. Satan has been defeated and the reign of sin overthrown. But the sinful nature resorts to a sort of guerrilla warfare to lead us into sin. This results in the struggle between the Spirit and the sinful nature which Paul wrote about: "For the sinful nature desires what is contrary to the Spirit, and the Spirit what is contrary to the sinful nature. They are in conflict with each other" Galatians 5:17.

(Reprinted by permission of NavPress, Colorado Springs, CO. © 1978 by The Navigators. All rights reserved.)

2. The first foe makes us vulnerable; the second takes advantage of that vulnerability. Study John 15:18-21 and I John 2:15-17. How would you identify this hindrance to Christian living?

The predominance of a world-view/world-system opposed to God.

The bleak side of human nature perpetuates a system of values and behavior diametrically opposed to the tenets of Christianity. In one sense, what the Bible calls the "world" is a corporate expression of the nature of the individual who doesn't belong to Christ.

3. Briefly, what are some concrete evidences, or expressions, of the world's value system in our day?

Rejection of authority, absolute truth, & morals; Tolerance.; All truths of equal value Unable to know anything.

4. Your third foe is an expert advertiser who glamorizes his commodities, and makes attractive appeals to your old nature. Glance at I Peter 5:8, 9 and Ephesians 6:10-13. This powerful foe is _____Satan_____. In the next part of the lesson, you'll zero in on this third foe.

A Devilish Character

Your scouting report on opponents of the Christian life now includes a sketch of three separate foes. The third, though, deserves a closer look. To be effective against him, you must scrutinize his characteristics and game strategies. The Bible calls him *Satan* (which means "adversary") or *Devil* (which means "slanderer"). By observing his game plan against Jesus (in Mt. 4:1-11) you can learn what God wants you to know about Satan's strategy.

Right before launching His public ministry, Jesus was confronted by Satan in the wilderness. Satan wanted Jesus to bypass the cross. He flung three separate temptations at the Lord. Read the temptation narrative three separate times. Analyze the data you observe, and write answers to these study questions:

1. What were the three temptations flung at Jesus?

Turn stones into bread (provide food inependent of God
Have power independent of God
To gain possessions independent of God

2. What character traits and strategies of Satan can you glean from the passage? (Get out your spiritual magnifying glass and look for things implied by the details in the passage. Not all the answers are direct statements about Satan. For instance, what does the fact that he approached Jesus three separate times, instead of once, say about our opponent?)

He doesn't give up; He's very crafty;
He was knowledgable (God, scripture, God's
plan for Jesus); He's determined;

54

He's very wise (comes at Jesus' weakest point & beginning of ministry)

The Winning Team

Though it's crucial to acknowledge our arch rival, and though we never want to underestimate his power, this study shouldn't inject a bleak, pessimistic attitude into our minds. Christianity is warfare, but our Commander-in-Chief has provided weapons of warfare guaranteeing ultimate victory. We aren't left to our own meager resources in our daily struggles against Satan. Paul encouraged the Corinthians with these words: "For though we live in the world, we do not wage war as the world does. The weapons we fight with are not the weapons of the world. On the contrary, they have divine power to demolish strongholds" (II Cor. 10:3, 4).

1. Let's shift our attention back to the temptation narrative, and notice how Jesus Himself employed one of these spiritual weapons. Precisely how did He combat Satan? (State your answer in a timeless way, so it will represent a means of combat available to believers of all eras.)

He stood against Satan by submitting to the authority of God & battling the lies of Satan w/the truth of God.

2. Three times Jesus quoted from the Book of Deuteronomy. Put these Old Testament quotes under the microscope of your mind for a moment. What is unique, or meaningful, about the way He used Scripture to defeat Satan? How is Jesus' manner of using Scripture applicable to us today?

Each verse Jesus used related to the specific type of temptation he was facing. When we're harrassed by Satan, we can read scriptures that relate to the area of the attack

55

Work Power

You've seen Jesus demonstrate how the Holy Spirit uses the written Word of God as a weapon against Satan. We have the same weapon at our disposal. Though Satan is strong, Christ's power is greater. And we tap into His power when we discipline ourselves to study His Word.

One ongoing discipline that many believers find helpful is Scripture memory. When you memorize Scripture you continually add to your stockpile of ammunition to use against Satan. It's like providing more fuel for the Holy Spirit to use when combating compromising situations that crop up from day to day.

Over the next couple of days, memorize Psalm 119:11: "I have hidden your word in my heart that I might not sin against you." Imagine—here is a memory verse that actually tells why we should memorize Scripture!

Overexposure

We've concluded that temptation demands a positive antidote: consistent application of God's Word. It's equally important, on the other hand, to restrict our exposure to things that drag us down spiritually. The battle against the sinful nature, the world's value system, and Satan cannot be won if we expose ourselves to their influence.

Here's a down-to-earth principle for daily spiritual victory: *Don't flirt with opportunities to sin.* When possible, don't expose yourself to things that make you weak. Just as we must say "yes" to positive influences, we must say "no" to potentially negative influences. Author Calvin Miller put it this way: "Our resistance to the secular is a matter of diet."

Pastor Charles Swindoll, in *Three Steps Forward, Two Steps Back* (Thomas Nelson Publishers), piggybacks on Miller's insight. Here's what he says about exposing ourselves to questionable influences:

Do not try to peacefully coexist with temptation. . . . If you are weakened by certain kinds of music, you are playing into the hands of Satan himself to listen to it. If you're weakened by certain motion pictures that bring before your eyes things that build desires within you that you can't handle, then you're not counteracting sin and temptation. You're tolerating it. You're fertilizing it. You're prompting it.

If the newsstand is something you can't handle, stay away from it! Quit clucking your tongue and shaking your head as you linger over the pages. If you're weakened by relationships with certain people, abstain from them. . . . You are a fool if you know what weakens you but feed on it anyway. There's a name for folks who linger and try to reason with lust: victim.

Taking Stock

It's unrealistic to think that we can remove ourselves from all tempting situations. Let's not use that fact as a rationalization, though. What is the Holy Spirit saying to you on this point? Are there avenues of ungodly influence that you're unwisely exposing yourself to? Are you exposing yourself to media sources that make it harder to live a holy life? Are you entangled in any social or business relationships that weaken your resistance to sin?

Those are extremely personal questions that only you can answer. If you sense God's convicting power in this regard, spend some time in prayer right now. And write down in the space below what you feel He is telling you to do. (You will NOT be asked to share this information during the next group session.)

_____

_____

_____

_____

8

CONVERSING WITH GOD

In *Growing Strong in the Seasons of Life,* Chuck Swindoll wrote about a home he visited on a winter evening. Above the log-stuffed, crackling fireplace hung this thought-provoking statement:

If your heart is cold, my fire cannot warm it.

As we walk with the Lord through the various seasons of life, how do we keep our hearts warm? What shelters that inward glow of faith from the inevitable breezes of rough cirucmstances and Satanic opposition? When the embers do begin to fade, what can rekindle the flame?

Getting Close

The answer is so basic that we take its heartwarming potential for granted: *prayer.* Regular communication with the Lord won't isolate us from the cold, harsh realities of life. But it can insulate us, as we tap the resources of the indwelling Holy Spirit.

Prayer is a discipline: a consciously chosen course of action that plugs us into the flow of God's grace and power. It is one of the spiritual weapons that equips us for battle against the foes of our faith (II Cor. 10:3, 4). Most importantly, though, it's a means of getting to know God better. As we spend time with Him through prayer and His Word, a more intimate level of relationship develops. The fire in our heart flickers out only when we fail to nurture that relationship with Him.

An incident from the life of D. L. Moody illustrates this ultimate purpose of prayer. One day his five-year-old boy creeped into his study, where Mr. Moody was writing. Somewhat perturbed about the interruption, Moody gruffly asked, "Well, what do you want?"

"Nothing, Daddy," his son replied. "I just wanted to be where you are."

The boy wasn't after a particular favor. He desired only companionship.

See how well you have grasped this overarching perspective. The ultimate purpose of prayer is:

To maintain a close relationship with
God and keep the fire going

The Model Prayer

Dotted throughout the Bible are meaty verses on the subject of prayer. We could put the spotlight on Bible personalities who prayed fervently, such as Elijah, Nehemiah, David, and Paul. We could dissect the instructions on prayer that Paul and Peter gave to young Christians in their letters. Since we have to be extremely selective, though, let's zero in on what Christ taught about prayer in Matthew 6:9-13.

Before you delve into these verses, let's set the stage. In Matthew 6:1-18, Jesus is warning listeners not to practice their righteousness merely to be noticed by those around them. In the realms of giving, praying, and fasting, He tells them to make God—not other people—their audience. In this context, He offered a prayer which He intended to serve as a timeless model for praying. From the words He used in this prayer, we can extract guidelines for our own prayer times.

Read Matthew 6:9-13 three times, then write down answers to these questions:

1. How did Jesus address God?

as Father

59

2. Why is that title significant? What does it suggest? (Read Jn. 1:12 and Rom. 8:15-17 to prod your thinking in response to this question.)

It points out the close-knit relationship we have with our Heavenly Father. We can approach God, knowing He cares for us.

3. What specific concerns did Jesus mention in His prayer?

God's glory, His kingdom coming, His will being done on earth, provision of daily needs a forgiving heart, victory over temptation + satan

4. How would you classify, or categorize, this list of concerns? What different types of concerns are included?

I. God (His person, kindom, + will)
II. Us (our material needs, need of forgiveness, + need of spiritual strength

5. How does Jesus' list of concerns compare with, or differ from, the concerns Christians most often take to God?

It's a prayer for God to work in our lives + in His world, not just to give us a bunch of things

6. As a wrap-up to your study of Matthew 6:9-13, answer this question: What different kinds of prayer is Jesus validating and encouraging?

adoration, confession, supplication,

7. The most meaningful insight about prayer that I gleaned from this passage is:

It's more about God + His plan than me and my plan

Four Kinds of Prayer

Christians have used various kinds of "helps" to guide them in their praying. Many have benefited from a useful tool which describes four different kinds of, or reasons for, prayer. This tool employs the acronym ACTS:

Adoration
Confession
Thanksgiving
Supplication

Adoration is praising God for who He is. When we express adoration in a prayer, we mention one or more divine qualities that set God apart from our imperfect humanness (the perfection of: holiness, power, justice, love, faithfulness, etc.). David wrote, "I will exalt you, my God the King; I will praise your name for ever and ever" (Ps. 145:1).

1. One quality of God that I'm particularly sensitive to this week is:

_____

Confession involves acknowledgement of the sin that the Holy Spirit exposes in our lives. We review the day gone by, and ask the Lord to show us where we strayed from His will. The term "confess" means "to agree with." We agree with God that a particular attitude or act was wrong, *and* we agree that Jesus' death on the cross paid the penalty for that sin. John assured his Christian readers with these words: "If we confess our sins, he is faithful and just and will forgive us our sins and purify us from all unrighteousness" (I Jn. 1:9).

2. Failing to confess our sins hinders the efficacy of our other prayers. Read Isaiah 59:1, 2. Summarize its time-less truth in your own words:

If we don't deal with the sin in our lives, we can't **61** maintain a relationship with God.

Take several minutes to replay the last 24 hours in your mind. Recall the family conversations, business transactions, attitudes toward people and circumstances. Is the Holy Spirit shining His spotlight on anything that needs to be confessed?

Thanksgiving is expressing gratitude to the Lord for things He has done (such as answered prayers, material provision, comfort during a trial). Whereas adoration focuses on His character, thanksgiving illuminates His deeds. "Give thanks in all circumstances, for this is God's will for you in Christ Jesus" (I Thess. 5:18).

3. List three specific things the Lord has done for you in recent weeks.

_____

_____

_____

Supplication is making requests to God. We're free to request things for ourselves, and trust God for the answer (whether it's yes, no, or wait). And we're encouraged to make requests on behalf of others. That's called "intercession."

4. Look up Philippians 4:6, 7, and answer the following:

What undesirable mindset can be relieved by the habit of making personal requests? _Worry_

What phrase from the text describes the scope of the requests we can bring to the Lord?

"in everything"

The result of making my requests known to God is:

peace

A specific request I have for God this week is:

_____

_____

5. Now turn to Ephesians 6:18, 19. What does the *context* of these verses suggest as a motive for intercession? (To answer, skim Eph. 6:10-17.)

the attack of satan

_____

In verse 19, Paul requested prayer for a fruitful ministry. Are you praying on a regular basis for your ministry, as well as the ministries of others in this LAMP course? For the pastoral staff of your church? For missionaries supported by your church?

Jot down the names of at least three individuals whose ministries you'll pray for at least weekly:

_____

_____

By the way, don't isolate these four kinds of prayer from one another. They become an effective devotional tool when you incorporate each kind into the same "quiet time" with God. You begin your prayer time with adoration, move to confession, then proceed to thanksgiving and supplication. Disciplined use of the ACTS formula will keep your prayers balanced. You won't fall into the rut of always approaching God for the same reason.

Easier Said Than Done

To talk about prayer, and to study the subject, is easier than praying! Your application of this lesson is to practice the ACTS method previously explained, and to share it with someone else.

First, set aside 20-30 minutes exclusively for this prayer time in your own life. Use the responses written in the previous section of the workbook as you proceed through the four steps. (For instance, you wrote down one quality of God that you're sensitive to this week. Praise Him as you meditate on this attribute. Confess any sins exposed by the Holy Spirit. Thank the Lord for the three things you listed that He has done for you. Give Him one or more personal requests, then pray for the ministries of the three people whose names you jotted down.) Resolve to use the ACTS tool at least once each week.

The day and time slot I will reserve each week for this period of prayer is:

_____

Second, think of a new Christian outside your study group. This could be an individual you've recently led to the Lord, or someone in another city whom you knew before you relocated. Make it a point to share the ACTS tool with another person within one week. In addition to helping the other person in his or her walk with the Lord, you will also benefit! Whatever content you verbalize or write to someone else, you yourself will retain for a longer period of time.

Be especially open to communicating it in a letter. You can sustain a relationship and exercise a ministry of encouragement despite the miles that separate you from old friends. View letter writing as a "first-class" ministry!

The person I can share the ACTS formula with is:

_____

To follow through on this goal, I will have to:

_____

_____

9

GETTING HELP
FROM GOD'S WORD

It happened years ago in Boston. Authorities discovered the bodies of two elderly women in their small apartment. An autopsy revealed the cause of death: malnutrition. The ladies had been on a meager diet for so long that their bodies gradually wasted away. "Victims of poverty," someone declared.

But a surprising discovery reversed that conclusion. Hidden in their mattresses, and sewn up in pillows and draperies, was nearly $200,000 in cash! Whether the ladies forgot about the money, or were afraid to go out of the apartment, no one knows. Either way, they died because they didn't use available resources to meet their need for food.

Food for the Christian

Most Christians who hear that story will shake their heads at such an inexcusable tragedy. Yet they slowly *starve themselves spiritually* by not feeding on the Word of God. An evangelist took a survey of several hundred young Christians. He asked how many had a daily time of devotional reading from the Bible. *Only three percent said they did!* Failing to take nourishment from God's Word will lead to spiritual malnutrition. Such neglect saps our vigor and endangers our spiritual health. Even the Holy Spirit used the analogy of food to describe the benefits of Bible study. He called it "pure milk" (I Pet. 2:2) and "solid food" (Heb. 5:14). It provides fuel for daily Christian living.

In Lesson 6 we learned that it's our responsibility to *pursue* holiness. God meets and empowers us as we choose to use the various means of growth He has established. In addition to prayer, one of those means of spiritual growth is reading God's Word. Digesting its morsels of truth inevitably adds weight and muscle to our spiritual frame. In the next few pages, you'll learn more about the Bible, and practice a simple method of digging into it.

Why the Bible Was Written

The concept of divine revelation was explained earlier in this course. "To reveal" means to tell or to show others information that otherwise they wouldn't have. What we tell or show others is called a revelation. Whereas most religions begin with humankind's attempt to find God, Christianity began with God's initiative. He attempted to reach and to restore persons by revealing Himself to them. Two main avenues of His revelation are the living Word (Jesus Christ), and the written Word (the Bible).

In II Timothy 3:16, Paul insisted that Scripture is *inspired* by God. The word inspiration, as applied to the Bible, means that its words were "breathed out by God." Though He employed the unique personalities and writing styles of human authors, the Holy Spirit guided each word that originally formed our Old and New Testaments. That's why Christians elevate this Book. Though it contains 66 separate books, written by more than 40 different human authors over a period of 1500 years, it's the only piece of literature that God has inspired as a means of revelation.

1. Let's see how firm a grip you have on the last two paragraphs. In your own words, answer this question:

Why does Christianity place so much emphasis on the Bible?

_____

_____

_____

2. When He inspired people to write the various books of the Bible, God had specific purposes in mind. In one sense, these purposes could be stated in the form of results that God wants to accomplish through the Bible. Probe the following sets of references. Jot down an overarching purpose for the Bible suggested by each; or, you may view what you write as results the Lord wants His Word to achieve in our lives.

Luke 24:44-46; John 5:39 _____

_____

_____

John 20:30, 31; I John 1:1-4 _____

_____

_____

Jeremiah 26:2, 3; Psalm 119:9, 11 _____

_____

_____

II Timothy 3:15-17 _____

_____

_____

Perspectives on Bible Study

There's a lot more we could say about the doctrine of the Bible. Right now, though, we want to shift the focus from theory to practice. It's almost time for you to practice a simple but effective approach to devotional Bible study. Nothing will motivate you to feed regularly on God's Word like a taste of its delicacies! First, let's go over a few guidelines to keep in mind as you delve into God's Word. Then we'll describe a concrete method for you to use.

BEGIN YOUR TIME OF BIBLE STUDY WITH PRAYER. Remember the lesson on the Holy Spirit? He is the One who illumines your mind, who helps you comprehend spiritual principles and see the applications for your life. Make the Psalmist's prayer your own: "Open my eyes that I may see wonderful things in your law" (Ps. 119:18).

EXAMINE YOUR LIFE TO MAKE SURE NO UNCONFESSED SIN BLOCKS YOUR COMMUNICATION WITH GOD. Isaiah wrote, "Your iniquities have separated you from your God; your sins have hidden his face from you, so that he will not hear" (Isa. 59:2). And David testified, "When I kept silent, my bones wasted away through my groaning all day long. For day and night your hand was heavy upon me; my strength was sapped as in the heat of summer" (Ps. 32:3, 4). Jesus' death gives you the right to enter God's presence and admit any sin spotlighted by the Holy Spirit. "If we confess our sins, he is faithful and just and will forgive us our sins and purify us from all unrighteousness" (I Jn. 1:9).

ANYTIME YOU READ A PASSAGE OF SCRIPTURE, HAVE THE EYE OF AN EAGLE! Be observant. We often gloss over words and details that offer timeless principles for living, or encouraging truths. An old Indian asked a stranger if he had seen the man who had stolen his guns. During the conversation, the Indian went on to say that the robber was young, short, heavy, and spoke with an Eastern accent. "You must have gotten a good look at him!" said the stranger.

"No," the Indian replied. "I never saw him. I know he's young because his footprints in the snow were crisp and showed no signs of dragging feet. He's short, because I found a box that he stood on in order to reach the guns. I know he's heavy because his footprints sank deep into the snow. And I figure he has an Eastern accent because he wore shoes instead of cowboy boots."

That's being observant! He analyzed the facts and came to logical conclusions. The Holy Spirit can help you do that when you study God's Word.

BE WILLING TO OBEY WHATEVER YOU OBSERVE. The content of God's Word is a means to an end, not an end in itself. God is concerned with our *response* to knowledge. Let's not become Biblically educated at the expense of our obedience. James put it this way: "The man who looks intently into the perfect law that gives freedom, and continues to do this, not forgetting what he has heard, but doing it—he will be blessed in what he does" (Jas. 1:25).

Sampling God's Menu

Here's a basic principle of investigation, applicable to "private eyes" as well as to students of the Bible: *I am more likely to find something if I am looking for it!*

When you read a passage of Scripture, make it a habit to look for certain things, and you're less likely to miss them. Below is a series of questions to help you read God's Word with a slant toward personal application. You can use these questions with almost any short segment of Scripture (usually a chapter or less). Of course, you won't necessarily find an answer to every one of these questions in every passage you read. However, most passages will offer answers to at least some of the questions. Also, the questions aren't necessarily mutually exclusive. An answer to one might also fit as an answer to another.

Let these nine questions serve as your utensils, and start feeding on God's Word right now. Everyone in your *Welcome to the Church* study group is going to practice this method on the same passage: Philippians

4:4-20. And in your next meeting, group members will share their discoveries with one another.

Read Philippians 4:4-20 a couple of times, as a devotional Bible study. Then jot down your answers to as many of the following questions as possible:

1. What words, phrases, or ideas are repeated in this passage? What is the significance of this repetition?

_____

_____

2. What are the commands in this passage? Which ones represent a timeless command for all believers? Which command speaks most personally to me? Why?

_____

_____

_____

_____

_____

3. What can I learn from either the negative or positive example of personalities mentioned in the passage?

_____

_____

_____

4. What promises to claim can I find here?

_____

_____

5. What sin or shortcoming does the passage expose in my life?

_____

_____

_____

_____

6. What reasons for praising God are suggested by the content?

_____

_____

7. What truth or principle encourages me? Why?

_____

_____

_____

8. How should what I'm reading affect my prayer life?

_____

_____

_____

9. How does this passage increase my appreciation for Jesus Christ?

_____

_____

_____

Spread the Blessing

Resolve to follow through on two things: (1) Share with a friend (face-to-face, or over the phone) one meaningful insight from your study of Philippians 4:4-20. What you share may be used by the Lord to encourage or sustain someone this week. Also, you want the other person to catch your enthusiasm for God's Word. (2) Think of someone with whom you can share the nine devotional questions introduced in this lesson. A lot of folks don't read the Bible because they don't know how to delve into it. Perhaps a neighbor has shown interest in spiritual things, and could benefit from this simple study approach. Or what about your own junior or senior higher? (Yet another alternative is to use these questions as the basis for a devotional series at home. You could gradually work through a short Bible book together, using the same list of questions each time you gather.)

10

LIFE IN THE FAMILY OF GOD

A Christian couple I know received the following poem from a friend in their church. The couple had experienced a rough year—job tensions, indecision over a career change, and financial strain. The writer expressed his feelings through the poem just prior to their out-of-state move.

I'm Wearing Your Skin

When your mind ponders what might have been,
  And despondently wonders why you can't win,
I also reflect on recent days
  And feel the effect of insensitive ways.

When you laugh, I do.
  When you weep, me too!
Through thick and thin,
  I'm wearing your skin.

When you feel insecure about a plan's revision,
  And wish you had fewer times of decision;
Then my situation becomes unglued,
  And my relationship to pain is renewed.

Whatever you feel, to some degree,
  Works its way into me.
Through your ups and downs, I'm spiritual kin—
  I'm wearing your skin!

Put yourself in the Florsheims of the recipients. If *you* received that poem, what words would describe your feelings?

_____

What effect might the poem have on your walk with the Lord? Why?

_____

_____

The relationship between the author and the couple, as reflected in the poem, provides a slice-of-life view of this week's theme. Though coming to Christ involves an individual decision that no one else can make for us, we grow in a corporate context called "the Church." God never meant for any Christian to go it alone. He meets and empowers us not only through prayer and Bible study, but also through other people who have entered into a relationship with Him.

God's Ideal

The Scripture passages that follow provide snapshots of God's ideal for the Church.

1. Read Ephesians 2:8-18. What is the foundation of, or basis for, unity and fellowship among Christians?

_____

2. Read Romans 12:4, 5; I Corinthians 12:12-27; and Ephesians 2:19-22. What specific figures, or analogies, does Paul employ to describe the Church? What is significant about these particular analogies?

_____

_____

_____

3. Consider the three passages again collectively. In 30 words or less, summarize what they teach about the Church.

_____

_____

_____

_____

4. What are some things that hinder the unity of and intimacy among believers in local congregations?

_____

_____

_____

_____

_____

How to Buck the Trend

As you pondered your response to question #4 perhaps you lamented the discrepancy between God's portrait for local churches, and the flawed picture that the world often sees. Let's face it. In an era of card-operated bank tellers and home computers, the quality of human relationships everywhere is eroding. Society's trend toward impersonalism sometimes drifts into the church. Richard Halverson, chaplain for the United States Senate, has said that relationships in some churches are like "balls on a billiard table. We ricochet around and bump into each other," he explains, "but rarely have any meaningful, lasting connections."

The fact that we fall short, though, is no reason to shrug off God's instructions on getting along. Despite our imperfections, no one has come up with a better idea than the Church for spreading the Gospel and nurturing believers to maturity. Let's decide to buck the trend toward impersonalism and superficiality, and strive to make the word "church" all that God intended it to be. Right now, let's view the concept of fellowship through the lens of Scripture, and discover Biblical guidelines for evaluating our experience of this means of growth.

To help us understand what it means to live as "parts of a body," or "members of a forever family," God has given specific commands to guide our Christian relationships. Most of these commands contain the phrase "one another" or "each other." Look up the following references and note the "one another" imperatives. This list is far from exhaustive, yet it offers some of the most crucial Bible references for evaluating relationships among believers. The verses help us see, in concrete terms, what "fellowship" looks like.

Galatians 6:2 _____

I Thessalonians 5:11 _____

II Corinthians 1:3-6 _____

Ephesians 4:2 _____

Romans 12:10 _____

Romans 12:13 _____

Romans 12:15, 16 _____

Romans 12:17-21 _____

Romans 15:7 _____

I Peter 4:10 _____

Colossians 3:12, 13 _____

Colossians 3:16 _____

Ephesians 6:18, 19 _____

Hebrews 10:24, 25 _____

1. Now mentally scrutinize this list of relational commands. Which of the practical expressions of fellowship do you feel are most lacking among Christians today? Why?

_____

_____

_____

2. Briefly describe a time in your Christian life when you were on the receiving end of one of the relational commands. Point out how the experience enhanced your walk with the Lord.

_____

_____

_____

_____

3. Which expression of fellowship do you most need to experience in your life right now? Why?

_____

_____

_____

Taking the Initiative

Someone has said, "Friendships are made—not born." That's true in the Body of Christ. If the Holy Spirit has exposed a need in your life for a deeper quality of fellowship, take the initiative to implement these commands within your church. Before long, others will become magnetically attracted to you.

Look over the various "one another" commands again. Ask the Lord to give you the name of one family or individual in your church who may have a need you can help meet (loneliness, a financial crisis, discouragement, etc.). The name the Lord brings to mind is:

_____

Now, decide which relational commands you need to obey in order to minister to that family or individual. Write them here:

_____

_____

_____

_____

_____

Specifically, how will you carry out these expressions of fellowship in the ensuing weeks? Describe your specific plans here:

_____

_____

_____

_____

_____

11

FITTING INTO
MY LOCAL CHURCH

Here's how one young person described the New Testament teaching on the Church and Christian fellowship:

God created me with missing parts . . . and He put those parts in other people called "Christians."

I like that! What a down-to-earth way of explaining the *interdependence* that believers have with one another.

The Church Where You Are

In the last lesson, you noted that the universal Church is called "the Body of Christ," and the "family of God." Also, you examined concrete Biblical evidences, or descriptions, of Christian fellowship. A series of "one another" commands helped you see more vividly the kind of relationships God has planned for people in the local church. You saw that a vibrant walk with the Lord, and a successful warfare against foes of the faith, aren't possible apart from meaningful involvement with other Christians.

Now let's narrow the focus a bit. The subject of this lesson is still "life in the family of God," but let's shine the spotlight on the local congregation where you are now. Let's probe some of the magnetic features of your church, and potential avenues for involvement.

Accentuate the Positive

No local congregation of believers is without flaws. Your pastoral staff would be the first to admit that no single cell in the Body of Christ has peaked in efficiency. That doesn't mean a congregation should excuse mediocrity, or fail to make ministry adjustments that can increase effectiveness. It's simply an admission of reality.

On the other hand, no matter how tainted we are, the local church is still God's primary agency for fulfilling His redemptive plan in the world. It is the primary God-intended avenue for worship, Bible instruction, fellowship, and training for ministry.

In *How to Begin the Christian Life* (Moody Press), George Sweeting summarizes:

According to the Word of God, the Church is a permanent, divine institution that shall never be destroyed (Mt. 16:18). One of the problems of the Church is that it is made up of people like you and me. The Church is a divine institution, founded by Jesus, but it is also a human institution. It is not a hothouse operating under ideal conditions in a controlled atmosphere. It is an organized group of imperfect saints, all of whom have faults and weaknesses.

Because God has chosen to work through local congregations, almost every church has features that attract certain people to it. These strengths, or magnetic qualities, deserve more attention than they receive. It's natural to react to imperfections, yet take the positive element for granted. In this first phase of your assignment, we want to increase your appreciation for the things your church and its leaders are doing right.

1. What initially attracted you to the church you are now attending?

_____

_____

_____

2. Specifically, what facets of your church's overall ministry has the Lord used to aid your personal spiritual development (and that of other members of your family)? (Think of programs, agencies, and groups spawned by the church.)

---

3. What contributions of your pastoral staff do you most appreciate?

How Do I Fit In?

Henry G. Bosch tells what happened when a customer in a small store discovered that the slow-moving clerk wasn't around one morning:

"Where's Eddie? Is he sick?"

"No," answered the store owner. "He doesn't work here anymore."

"Oh . . . have you filled the vacancy yet?" the customer inquired.

"No, ma'am. That's the problem with Eddie. He didn't leave no vacancy!"

Believers in a local congregation should be so involved in the church's life that they leave a vacancy when they move away or die. If we're contributing to the varied ministries of a church, we'll be missed by somebody when we're no longer around. The vacancy we leave behind may be a teaching position, a committee assignment, or some informal, behind-the-scenes role.

To dig up the Biblical roots of this "everyone is a minister" concept is beyond the scope of this lesson.

That's reserved for another LAMP course, *Welcome to Your Ministry*. For now, let's just acknowledge that Christian ministry isn't a spectator sport. Benches and bleachers in the church are strictly man made. Rather than sit and watch an elite few perform, all believers need to pitch in and involve themselves in the work of a church. This is God's will for the local church. Without such involvement, progress toward spiritual maturity is hampered.

Grow by sharing

Consider the following ways to fit into the work of your church. This list is far from exhaustive, but perhaps it will spur your thinking.

FITTING IN THROUGH CHURCH MEMBERSHIP. Most local churches maintain a list of individuals who have officially united with the congregation. Persons on this membership roll often enjoy privileges and responsibilities not available to nonmembers. In most cases, nonmembers cannot vote on important decisions during congregational business meetings, or serve in key leadership or teaching positions. Nonmembers can take advantage of and support the church's ministries to some extent, but their participation is limited in scope.

The person who minimizes the significance of church membership unwittingly impedes his or her own spiritual growth. Becoming a member is the ultimate way to acknowledge the interdependence of those in the body of Christ. It's a public way of declaring, "This is my church. I can't grow without receiving from and giving to others in this congregation." To become a member means committing myself to the people in the church, to the work of the church, and to the head of the church—Jesus Christ.

I Cor 1 Pet

Precise procedures and qualifications for membership differ among local churches. If you aren't a member, is God's Spirit nudging you in that direction? If so, contact your pastor this week.

Questions I have about the church before I decide to join:

_____

_____

_____

_____

The requirements for membership in the church I'm attending are:

_____

_____

_____

_____

As the previous paragraphs suggest, church membership is important because:

_____

_____

FITTING IN THROUGH REGULAR ATTENDANCE AT SERVICES OF THE CHURCH. Christian living has both private and corporate dimensions. We need private times of prayer, Bible study, and worship. Yet in order to be spiritually well rounded, we need to experience the same disciplines in a corporate context. John Wesley wrote, "The Bible knows nothing of solitary religion." D. L. Moody said, "Church attendance is as vital to a disciple as a transfusion of rich, healthy blood to a sick man." These great leaders were emphasizing the need for public assemblies of Christians.

Though the Lord can teach us through personal Bible study, we need the spiritual food dished out by the pastor, by our Sunday School teachers, and home Bible study leaders. Our diet of God's Word is woefully inadequate without the insights of others. In the sphere of public worship, we're strengthened spiritually through singing, hearing testimonies of God's work in others' lives, and participating in communion. Worshipping corporately reminds us that other people share similar beliefs, joys, and struggles. That's why the author of Hebrews wrote, "Let us not give up meeting together, as some are in the habit of doing, but let us encourage one another—and all the more as you see the Day approaching" (Heb. 10:25). What are some specific benefits you've experienced as a result of attending the services of your church?

_____

_____

_____

FITTING IN THROUGH STEWARDSHIP OF TIME, ENERGY, ABILITIES, AND FINANCIAL CONTRIBUTIONS TO THE WORK OF THE CHURCH. Remember that what we give financially to God's work is merely a by-product of a "total life commitment" to Him. Before the Macedonian believers opened their wallets, they "gave themselves first to the Lord" (II Cor. 8:5). God wants you to have impact on others through frugal stewardship of all the resources He has given you. As Paul suggested in Ephesians 2:10, he saved you for the purpose of ministry: "We are God's workmanship, created in Christ Jesus to do good works, which God prepared in advance for us to do."

A Closer Look at Giving

If we believe the local church is God's primary agency for ministry, then we'll give a portion of our income to keep it functioning. Take several minutes to read II Corinthians 8 and 9. Paul is encouraging the believers in Corinth to send an offering to the famine-stricken congregation in Jerusalem.

1. Note verses 1 and 12 in chapter 9. What word did Paul use to describe giving? Why do you think he used this word?

_____

2. Note 8:1-9. What examples of giving did Paul mention? What impresses you about these examples?

_____

_____

_____

3. Examine 8:2-4 and 9:7. What phrases from the text reflect the attitude God looks for in a giver?

_____

_____

_____

4. Focus on 9:6-11. What phrases directly from the text show God's responsiveness to a giving person?

_____

_____

_____

5. In addition to II Corinthians 9:12-15, skim the following references: Matthew 6:19, 20, 25-33; Philippians 4:14-19; and I Timothy 6:7. What additional motivations for a giving life-style can you glean from these verses?

_____

_____

_____

6. Based on what I've read in God's Word, I need to make the following adjustments in my giving to the local church:

_____

_____

_____

In your next group meeting, you may be given a CHRISTIAN SERVICE INVENTORY form. On it will be listed a wide spectrum of service opportunities, skills, age-level ministries, and so forth. You'll have a chance to ponder your past experiences, areas of burden or interest, and God-given abilities. Then you'll check off areas for possible future involvement in your church. Filling out the form will not obligate you or the church at this present time. It merely serves as a tool for leaders who try to match needs in the church's ministries to the abilities and desires of persons in the congregation. Right now, pause and ask the Lord to guide you when you complete the service inventory form.

We've covered just four basic avenues of involvement in your church. The longer you attend, the more aware you'll become of specific ways to plug into its service outlets.

Truly Grateful?

Often we feel grateful for a particular program or person, but fail to express that gratitude. This week:

Write your pastor a "thank-you" note for his leadership. Mention a particular aspect of his ministry that you appreciate: long hours of sermon preparation; ability as a counselor; availability during a crisis, etc. And whether or not he is directly involved in it, mention one of the ministries listed in #2 under "Accentuate the Positive." Many members of a congregation call or write the pastor only when they have a personal problem or complaint. Dare to be different!

Send a "thank-you" note to one other person who is investing time and energy in one of the ministries you listed in response to #2 under "Accentuate the Positive." (Sunday school teacher or superintendent? Prayer chain coordinator? Youth Director?)

12

DON'T KEEP IT
TO YOURSELF

The Dead Sea is a lake occupying the southern end of the Jordan River Valley. Its northern tip rests not far from the city of Jerusalem. This sheet of greenish, salty water is 11 miles across at its widest point, and almost 50 miles long. The water itself is marked by a distinctively bitter taste, and a nauseous smell.

Have you ever wondered why it's called the "Dead" Sea? The water is so intensely saline, and contains so many minerals such as bromide and sulphur, that few living things can survive in it. The water houses these minerals and can't support many life forms like a normal lake for one basic reason: *the Dead Sea has inlets, but no outlets.* Millions of tons of water—from the Jordan and several smaller streams—flow into the basin daily. But no streams flow from it to other parts of the country. This salty sea would be fresh or only mildly saline had it an outlet: but the landlocked basin in which it rests in that hot and arid climate serves as a gigantic evaporating pan. Flooding is prevented because the dry heat rapidly evaporates the water.

This fact about the Dead Sea reflects a truth of Christian living: we need to construct outlets so that whatever blessings flow into our lives, eventually refresh others as well. Our lives aren't as fresh, reproductive, and attractive if what we're learning and experiencing isn't channeled toward others with whom we have contact. The time-worn maxim, "impression without expression equals depression" captures the idea.

Looking Back

In this final lesson of the course, you'll reconsider some of the impressions God's Word and your LAMP study group has made on your life. And you'll think through some ways to express what you've learned in relation to others. By constructing outlets for what you've been learning, you'll stay spiritually alive, and irrigate the hearts of others who thirst for God.

Take several minutes to reflect on this *Welcome to the Church* course. Consider what you've gleaned from this workbook and its assignments; the supplementary insights provided by your study group leader; and the benefit of relationships with other learners. To jog your memory of specific subjects you've covered, skim the lesson titles and put your mental finger on the main thrust of each lesson. Then write a short paragraph to complete each sentence that follows. Bible studies should *form* you—not just *inform* you. What you write will indicate ways in which you've been formed by God.

1. One new (I've-never-thought-of-that-before) insight about Christian living that I've reaped from this course is:

_____

_____

2. Perhaps the most encouraging experience or truth from the past twelve weeks is:

_____

_____

3. The most convicting thing I learned, which exposed the need for a significant change in my life, was:

_____

_____

4. Overall, the lesson from this course that left the biggest impact on my life was:

_____

because:

_____

_____

5. In response to the emphasis on "ministry" woven throughout the curriculum, the most satisfying occasion in which I used lesson content to serve others was:

_____

_____

Investment Opportunity

As you ponder God's input into your life through this course, let the following Scripture passage speak to you regarding stewardship of what you've learned: Matthew 25:14-30. (Read it a couple of times.)

1. In 25 words or less, summarize the timeless truth that Jesus is communicating:

_____

_____

_____

_____

2. The result of good stewardship of my resources is (v. 23):

_____

_____

Though the parable uses money as a case in point, it's a call for wise use of *all* God-given resources: time, abilities, knowledge, etc. We're responsible to invest them so the final yield will be greater than the amount received. The last thing the Lord desires is a doormat ability, or Bible knowledge that diminishes with time because it's "buried" as the talents in Jesus' parable. You've been handed something to manage. Will you hide it on a shelf, in the form of this workbook, or invest it in the lives of other new Christians, so its effects can be multiplied?

In one sense, you now have a greater responsibility before God than you had 12 weeks ago. You are now accountable for what you've learned! Jesus once put it this way: "From everyone who has been given much, much will be demanded; and from the one who has been entrusted with much, much more will be asked" (Lk. 12:48).

Use It or Lose It

At various points throughout the course, you were encouraged to share material from individual lessons. Ideas included nurturing relationships with non-Christians and sharing the plan of salvation with them; writing notes of encouragement; going over devotional tools such as the nine Bible study questions and ACTS prayer formula with a new believer; and conveying an attribute of God through either structured or informal conversation with a child in the home. Each time you followed through on suggestions of this sort, you constructed an outlet for the flow of blessings that you received from God through the course.

Now that the course is almost over, don't stop looking for ways to pass along what you've learned. Ironically, the more you give it away, the more "ownership" you'll have of the material. In addition to communicating bits and pieces of information as needs and opportunities surface, consider ways to communicate the entire course systematically. Options include:

DISCIPLING ONE OTHER PERSON BY TAKING HIM OR HER
THROUGH THE WORKBOOK. The setting could be an office,
a restaurant, or the living room of your home. This
approach doesn't require you to serve as a teacher in
the public, formal sense. The main qualification is a
thoroughly completed workbook, and the zeal to see
another Christian grow in the Lord. Of course, the
other party would need a new, empty *Welcome to the
Church* workbook.

If this approach entices you, ask the Lord for the
name of someone at work, in your neighborhood, or
church. Jot down his or her name here _____ .

Broach the possibility with the person whose name
you wrote down. If he or she is willing to pay the price,
put your first meeting time on your planning calendar.

INVITING TWO OR THREE OTHER MARRIED COUPLES INTO
YOUR HOME FOR 12 ONCE-A-WEEK STUDY SESSIONS. (If you
aren't married, invite four to six other singles.) This
setting may require a bit more group leadership than
the one-on-one approach, but your role will primarily
be to facilitate discussion of the completed assignments. Your discussion-leading task still won't require
the formal teaching expertise of a more structured classroom setting. If the Lord nudges you to adopt this
approach, get a copy of the **Leader's Guide** for *Welcome
to the Church*. Skim each lesson plan for questions or
learning activities that you can adapt to the more informal learning atmosphere. (Alternative ideas: ladies,
mull over the possibility of a daytime study group with
several other women who don't work. Men, one on one
isn't the only context for discipling. Could you meet
with two or three guys at breakfast or lunch, instead of
just one?)

Think of contacts outside your local church as well as
within it. You may know neighbors or co-workers who
love the Lord, but who attend a church irregularly.
Names of couples or individuals you can take through
the workbook include:

_____ _____

_____ _____

_____ _____

TEACHING A CHURCH-SPONSORED CLASSROOM VERSION OF *WELCOME TO THE CHURCH*. As the Lord brings new people into your church, and members lead people to faith in Jesus Christ, this course will be offered again. The church needs a host of persons whom God has tabbed for group leadership roles. If God has implanted in you a desire to lead a group, and you're sold on the benefits of the course, pursue the matter. Talk to your current group leader about the possibility. Ask for feedback on your potential as a teacher. Also investigate the formal approval process or procedures required by your church for those in teaching positions.

There are three major ways a person learns to teach:

OBSERVATION. You learn to lead by being part of a study group that has a capable leader. Over a period of time, you observe and experience leadership skills and learning methods that you'll need to employ as a study group leader. Right now, concentrate on the leader you've had the past three months.

1. Specifically, what has this person modeled that you want to implement when you lead your own group?

_____

_____

_____

_____

_____

_____

2. What principles of group dynamics, or group life, have you experienced that you will want to incorporate in a class you lead?

_____

_____

_____

_____

_____

_____

TRAINING. Everyone needs to hone his or her God-given skills by participating in workshops and training courses. **Leader's Guides** are available for each LAMP course. LAMP also has an excellent training manual specifically designed to prepare study leaders to lead LAMP courses. Your church may provide other training opportunities for budding study group leaders. If not, express your desire for such training to someone on the pastoral staff.

3. I'd feel more comfortable as a group Study Leader if I could receive training in the following specific areas:

_____

_____

_____

_____

PRACTICE. The old "learn by doing" principle has been around a long time because it's true. It's impossible to acquire or polish teaching skills without practice. Hearing tapes and reading books on teaching are a supplement to—not a substitute for—hands-on experience. If you lack experience, ask a capable teacher of adults to participate in your first couple of classes, to offer you constructive feedback. Remember that the Lord will equip you for whatever He calls you to do (see II Cor. 3:1-6).

Resources

To supplement the observation, training, and practice which are essential to development as a LAMP Study Leader, digest one or more of the following books:

LeFever, Marlene. *Creative Teaching Methods* (David C. Cook Publishing Co.). Contains step-by-step directions for dozens of methods appropriate for use in adult classes.

Mayes, Howard and Long, James. *Can I Help It If They Don't Learn?* (Victor Books). Crisply written in a humorous, nontechnical style. Emphasizes teaching for life application.

Nyquist, John. *Leading Bible Discussion* (InterVarsity Press). Shows how to study Scripture inductively, and plan discussion-oriented group sessions based on the study insights. Includes excellent "how-to" tips on leading discussions.

Richards, Larry. *Sixty-Nine Ways to Start a Study Group and Keep It Growing* (Zondervan). Geared to home Bible study groups that meet for fellowship as well as Bible Study. Chock full of usable "team-building" ideas that help create a warm group atmosphere.

Zuck, Roy. *The Holy Spirit in Your Teaching: Revised and Expanded Edition* (Victor Books). Discusses the gift of teaching, and how divine/human elements work in tandem in the classroom.

Christian Service Inventory

Name _____

Address _____

_____

_____

Age _____ Phone _____

Occupation _____

Employer _____

Church Membership

☐ Nonmember ☐ Member for _____ years

Educational Background

List schools/areas of study

_____

_____

_____

_____

Types of leadership training or teacher training I've had
(secular or church related):

_____

_____

_____

Christian Service Background

Capacities in which I have served in a church, and number of years in each area:

_____

_____

_____

_____

_____

_____

Total number of years I have served in a local church:

_____

Christian ministry experiences outside the church program:

_____

_____

_____

_____

_____

My areas of interest and potential involvement at our church (if properly trained):

_____

_____

_____

_____

_____

_____